THE UNEMPLOYMENT BUDGET

YOUR FINANCIAL SURVIVAL PLAN

PATRICK MELLODY

ISBN: 978-1-936539-64-2

EBook cover by: Ryan Mellody Freelance
ryan_mellody@yahoo.com

EBook editing by: Chris O'Byrne
www.ebook-editor.com.

Special thanks to my author friends that spent hours reading, editing and guiding me.

Jan Siebold, author of superb children's books
www.jansiebold.com.

Bruce Eaton, author of *Concurring Your Financial Stress* and other fine books.
www.eatonresources.com.

Table of Contents

Chapter 1
So it hapened to you..1

Chapter 2
That's not the way we planned it!...3

Chapter 3
The Crisis Budget.
For when you need help today! 5

Chapter 4
The Unemployment Budget
May I have a receipt, please? 9

Chapter 5
Am I worth more dead than alive?..11

Chapter 6
Where am I? 13

Chapter 7
It's like finding new-found money! 15

Chapter 8
What is a variable expense and why should I care? 16

Chapter 9
What is the magic formula for spending and how do I size up?....................17

Chapter 10
You mean I don't get to spend it all? 19

Chapter 11
Clear off the kitchen table and put it all together...21

A Special Word to Returning and
Retired Military Men and Women...24

Referral Services 25

Faith-based Referral Services..26

All the forms in this book may be downloaded free at

Budgets That Work
www.budgetsthatwork.com/forms

For privacy, the names in this book have been changed.

Online Discussion

Join in the online discussion of this book by going to
twitter.com/#!/search/realtime/UnemploymentBudget.

To add to the discussion, simply add #UnemploymentBudget to the end of your tweet.
If you are completely new to Twitter, go to support.twitter.com and click on Twitter basics.
I will join in the discussion and I look forward to meeting all of you.

CHAPTER 1
SO IT HAPPENED TO YOU

You have been laid off, down-sized, right-sized, fired, or your employer locked the door because of the economy. You are upside down on your house value and the future is looking bleak. You need to survive and protect what you have left. You need a plan to ride out this economic storm. Bad things do happen to good people like you, but you don't have to be one of the casualties of this unemployment nightmare. In this short book you'll find two budgets—I'll walk you through both.

#1 The "Crisis Budget" If you are down to the wire financially and need to make quick but informed decisions, this is the budget you need. You can do this today!

#2 "The Unemployment Budget" This budget is more detailed and it will help you get more organized. You'll have a solid foundation on which you can not only survive, but be able to move forward. Your financial stress will be reduced and allow you to focus on finding your next job.

Each short chapter starts with a story of someone I have helped develop a budget over my past 17 years as a volunteer budget coach. Every story is unique and has a part to play in the budget process. Not everyone faced unemployment, but they all faced financial challenges so severe that it led them to talk to me, a total stranger, about how they spend their money. There is something to be learned from every story. At the end of each chapter you'll find a simple form to fill in that will help you on your way. If you are like me you dislike financial books that scold you for not doing everything perfectly all your life. I also dislike the ones that tell you to do this or that in a specific order which implies that you fit into a cookie cutter group. Let me tell you what I have found, unless you are in the small majority the last thing you want to do is create and live on a budget. The second last thing you want is some author telling you what to do as if you are a fifth grader. I respect you and what you are going through because I have been there also. If you're reading this book the motivation for you and your family to survive must be greater than the alternative. I congratulate you on making this step and applaud your efforts. You'll be happy to know that I wrote this book in a way which allows you to start where it is easiest for you. Getting started is the most important thing. We all have books collecting dust that we never finished, this one allows you to be in charge. Simply read the short chapters, look at the forms and do the easiest one first, then the next. Before you know it you'll have read some fun stories, completed all the forms and have everything you need to pull it all together in the final chapter. At the end of the stories and the activities you'll feel a sense of accomplishment and control. You'll know where you stand financially, how to survive unemployment and prepare for the future. As I mentioned, I have been where you are. I stared bankruptcy in the face, but because someone took the time to help me learn what is in this book, I survived. Thank you, Harry, this book is dedicated to you.

Here is what you can expect from this book:

- You'll have a complete understanding of where your money is going on a monthly basis.

- You'll know exactly how much you are over/under spending in every category of life—housing, food, auto, and so on. You'll also know how much you are over/under spending totally per month and what to do about it.

- You'll have "New-found Money" that was saved by adjusting your spending habits.

- You'll be provided a web site where you can download all the forms in this book for no charge.

- If you just have too many bills that you cannot pay, I'll provide solid contact information for a non-profit organization that I have recommended dozens of times. They will help you work out a debt management plan that will relieve your financial stress.

- You'll discover how to survive this temporary season of life.

Let's start with my own personal story. Hang on—it's going to be a bumpy ride.

CHAPTER 2
THAT'S NOT THE WAY WE PLANNED IT!

As I closed the door to my boys' bedroom I felt my heart sink. Tonight was to be the night that I told them, but I couldn't bring myself to do it. How could I tell them that we had to sell the house to pay bills and to keep from going bankrupt? They didn't even know what bills were. They wouldn't understand that we'd have to move back into an apartment and start over. All those boys knew is that they had a great life, a nice home with a pool in the back yard, and a group of friends at kindergarten. There was a new playground at the end of the street where they played daily with neighborhood friends. How did I ever let our finances slip this far? What happened along the way?

My wife and I found ourselves on a financial roller coaster and there was no way off. Our income had climbed steadily every year, similar to going up that first hill of a roller coaster. The car grabbed the chain that pulled us up the income hill. Click, click, click, we made more and spent more. Click, we bought a home, click, we bought better cars, a Disney vacation and more. The higher our income climbed the more we had to spend—and we did. We were not irresponsible people. We didn't spend extravagantly. The debt just slowly accumulated and piled up. I thought there would always be time for saving. One of the problems of climbing that first hill of the roller coaster is that you can't see what's on the other side. I knew we had reached the peak of that hill when I received a phone call informing me that the company I distributed for as a salesman lost their biggest customer, which meant that I did also. In that 60-second phone call my income was cut in half! For the first time I could now see what was in front of me as the roller coaster car crested the hill, leaned forward and I was looking straight down. The carload of debt I had amassed propelled us down the track with great momentum. I could not stop it if I tried. As our income plummeted my wife took a job waiting tables. I took a second job, but it still wasn't enough to slow us down. I took a weekend job. I didn't know if I was coming or going. I took a change of clothes with me in the morning, along with a bag lunch and dinner. I changed clothes between jobs in the men's room of a Holiday Inn. What a nightmare I had created! The ride was about to end and the finish was not looking pretty.

One night I was sitting at the kitchen table with a stack of bills and a less stacked checkbook. My wife walked by and I said, "Wouldn't it be nice just to get to zero?"

"What do you mean," she asked.

"Just to be at zero where we don't owe anyone anything. We wouldn't have much, but at least starting over again at zero would mean we could move forward."

A Pen and a Dunkin' Donuts Napkin

Our last-minute survival journey began with a pen and a Dunkin' Donuts napkin. One day I was driving down Walden Avenue in Buffalo, NY. I was listening to a radio program on finances. The guests' name was Larry Burkett. It was a very interesting show and at the end he said that his organization had free volunteer budget coaches that could help me survive my financial dilemma and get me back on the right track. Well, my roller coaster car was off the tracks and I was definitely all about free. As he read off his number, 1-800-722-1976, I frantically found a pen and a Dunkin' Donut napkin. I put the napkin on the center of the steering wheel and somewhat successfully driving the car with my knees at 45 miles per hour I wrote down the most important number of my life. When I got home from hunting for a full time job I called that number and they gave me the name of a man in Rochester, NY that would help me. His name was Harry. I called Harry and he offered to meet with my wife and me on a Saturday morning. I didn't really understand why someone would give up his Saturday morning for free, but we drove the 1½ hours to meet with him. I remember that we took the back roads so we didn't have to pay the "I Love NY" thruway tolls. Harry taught us the financial principles years of school never did. Harry led us through the same process that this book will lead you through. Our financial pressure began to decrease and yours will also.

The purpose of this book is to share with you what we have learned. I have now been a volunteer budget coach myself for over 17 years and I know first-hand what you are going through. I have helped others to survive and now it's your turn.

Here is how this book works. From coaching people of every age, income, and life stage I understand that no two people/couple are the same. I have learned to meet people where they are in life. As previously mentioned I've written this book in such a format that you can choose any chapter to begin. Some people like to look at each activity at the end of the chapters and start with the one that is easiest for them. That's fine. At least you can get started. Just keep the end result in mind: your survival and the relief of financial stress. Each of the remaining chapters has an activity for you to do. When you complete the chapters you'll have everything you need to put it all together. Let's begin. I'll join you at the last chapter to put it all together. It's worth starting today.

CHAPTER 3
THE CRISIS BUDGET.
FOR WHEN YOU NEED HELP TODAY!

Here is the Crisis Budget. You can print out this form at www.budgetsthatwork.com/forms.

THE CRISIS BUDGET

1) Calculate your monthly take-home income BEFORE the loss of any Job or Jobs.	2) Deduct the amount of take-home income lost.	3) Subtract Total #1 from Total #2 and see your monthly income before Unemployment and other assistance.	
Job 1 $	Job 1 $		
Job 2 $	Job 2 $		
Other income $	Other income $		
Other income $	Other income $		
Total #1 $	Total #2 $	$	Total #3

4) Enter your take-home income from:		
Unemployment	$	
Severance	$	
Food Stamps	$	
Other Assistance	$	
Other new income	$	
Total	$	Total #4

** Your New Monthly Spendable Income:	$	Total of #3 + #4

5) Monthly Food   Total $

Take out	$
Groceries	$

Monthly Housing   Total $

Mortgage or	$
Rent	$
Insurance	$
Taxes	$
Electric	$
Gas	$
Water	$
Garbage	$
All Phones	$
Internet	$
TV Plan	$
other	$

Monthly Auto   Total $

Payments	$
Gas&Oil	$
Insurance	$
License	$
Register	$
Repair	$
Other	$

6) Subtract your total Food, Housing and Auto expenses from your ** New Monthly Spendable Income $

This is what you have left over or are short after paying your Monthly Triangle Needs.

Print this form at www.budgetsthatwork.com/forms

From the book "The Unemployment Budget" Your financial survival plan by Patrick Mellody

You need to survive this crisis. Like a triangle you have three points to protect. You need to eat, have a place to live, and transportation. I'll help you list all your spending that falls into the triangle. After we accomplish that we'll list your other spending that falls outside the triangle. Hope is on the way because I will tell you about a service that will work with your creditors to reduce your interest rates and develop a long term repayment strategy. It's a non-profit organization that I've recommended dozens of times and they're fantastic! Your debts will not go away, they'll just become more manageable.

If you still have some form of medical insurance from a working spouse you're very lucky. If you don't and you can't afford COBRA coverage from your former employer, you must seek out help from your local county offices right away. Don't feel like a welfare case. When you were working you paid into these services. If you want to pay them back after you are on your feet again, that's fine, but they exist to help you through a rough time.

As you go through the Crisis Budget you'll most likely find that you can't pay all your bills in full with your current reduced income. If this is the case, you need to accept it and prioritize the funds you do have coming in so you and your family can eat, have a place to stay, and a mode of transportation to look for and secure your next job. You will find a new job. You will survive this temporary setback.

The Crisis Budget is only six steps and then you're done. You can do it.

As you look at the Crisis Budget Form you'll see:

1. Calculate your monthly take-home income BEFORE the loss of any job or jobs. This is to include all income from all family members whose income helped pay the household expenses. To find this figure look at everyone's last pay stub without severance included. Locate your net income. (after taxes, social security, medical and so on) Multiply the amount by 52 weeks and divide by 12 months which equals your monthly take-home income. If you were paid every two weeks, multiply by 26 and then divide by 12 months.

2. Deduct the amount of take-home income lost due to unemployment.

3. Subtract Total #1 from Total #2 and see your monthly income before Unemployment and other assistance.

4. Enter your take-home income from the sources listed. Add Total #3 and #4 together and place the amount in the box provided. This equals your New Monthly Spendable Income.

5. Fill in your Monthly Food, Housing and Auto expenses in the boxes provided. Total them in the boxes provided.

6. Now we need to deduct your food, transportation and housing totals from your New Monthly Spendable Income.

Remember that you may have to temporarily go back to the basics.

Food: Cut back to nutritious foods purchased on sale with coupons. Coupons are a pain, but they are the same as currency. Eating out, take-out and your local coffee spot may have to be temporarily cut back or eliminated. You can go back to the luxuries when you get your next job.

Housing: Housing costs include everything that is spent in the house. All phones, Internet, TV, utilities, taxes and your mortgage or rent. Again, cut out the luxuries for now. When you need to survive one phone that prospective employers can easily reach you on is fine. Life will go on with only having local channels with an antenna, and a thermostat change will not matter in the long run.

Transportation/Auto: Cut out unnecessary trips. Talk to your insurance agent about adjusting your coverage temporarily. If you have multiple cars, you may have to consider taking one off the road as long as it does not affect your ability to search for your next job. Please do not cut out the oil changes or anything to do with safety. I can't tell you how many people I spoke to that let their car run down and could not afford to replace it. The cheapest car you have is the one you own. If you live in a major city and don't own a car, protect the funds you spend for traveling by bus, subway, or taxi.

Also, if you are to survive, you should not add to your current debt. Do your best to live on what you have coming in. You'll only make things worse by going further into debt. Spend your money carefully and never pay retail price. Someone once said, "Money is like time, you only get to spend it once."

Now that you have completed the form you know how much it will cost to keep your Triangle protected. Your family's food, housing, and transportation are secure and hopefully there is some money left over. If you're facing major decisions in your life, you'll now know what it will take to survive this season of unemployment. If there's not enough income to cover your triangle, even after you have reduced your luxury expenses, don't give up hope. I know a non-profit organization that can help you. Either way, your next step, after you've completed at least this form, is to contact CredAbility. CredAbility is a non-profit organization that will help you create a DMP or Debt Management Plan. The DMP will address the debt obligations you may have trouble paying. Their web site is www.credability.org . Click on "Our Services" and then "Debt Management Plan". Watch the short video explaining the service. If you decide to work with them the remaining forms in this book will make the process go much faster. As I mentioned previously I have referred dozens of people to this organization and it helped them survive and then thrive. You can also call them at 1-800-251-2227. CredAbility also has services such as Foreclosure Prevention and if you're far short of even your basic needs, they offer Bankruptcy Education. Please exhaust all the referral services at the end of this book before considering bankruptcy. It's the last resort and unlike they say on TV it will not make all your problems go away, it will only create new ones. CredAbility is a non-profit agency but they do have an average charge of $35 to set up your account and a maximum charge of $50 if you have a lot going on that takes extra administrative time. It's the best money you'll ever spend and you'll save it back right away. CredAbility already has pre-approved arrangements with all the major credit card companies and lenders to lower your interest and payments. CredAbility does stress that they are not a debt settlement company. They suggest that you contact your creditors directly if you have funds available to settle your debt for a lower amount and close the account. They do not suggest paying some other TV-advertised company to do what you can do yourself. I do suggest that you build in emergency savings into your CredAbility plan. If you don't have savings, you'll fall into using credit again and we all know emergencies happen all the time.

So there you are. You now know what income you bring home, where to spend it first and hopefully what you have left over for other bills. You have a place to go for help with those remaining bills and additional counsel. No one has the power to erase all your debt and eventually we all have to pay back what we borrow. I hope you'll find that the information in this chapter will keep you going until you secure your next job.

CHAPTER 4
THE UNEMPLOYMENT BUDGET
MAY I HAVE A RECEIPT, PLEASE?

Now it's time to get into the "Unemployment Budget". This budget is made up of a series of forms that will help you get organized at a deeper level than the crisis budget. It all starts with "The Starbucks Couple", Mary and Roger.

One day I received a call from Mary. (Why is it the men never call?) Mary described a very familiar situation to me. She told me that some of their friends were now without a job and in deep financial trouble. Mary said that she and her husband Roger had recently talked. They decided that they should get ahead of the game in case one of them lost their job. Roger and Mary are a very busy young couple. They both have intense jobs plus there were children to pick up at daycare and a home to keep up. They had a generally crazy and hectic life. The day began at 6:00 a.m. and didn't stop until after they got the kids to bed at 8:00 p.m. They were totally exhausted. Life just went on day by whirlwind day. If they needed or wanted something, they just bought it. They weren't over-indulgent, they just didn't watch their spending very closely. Their massive debt accumulated slowly. They both started their marriage with school loans and credit card debt. They needed reliable vehicles, so they leased a car and a minivan. They bought more house than they should have, so they had a robust mortgage payment. Daycare costs were high and doctor expenses never ended. The list went on. Before they knew what happened expenses totaled up and money was now very tight. Sometimes tempers flared over who was spending the most. They had friends go down this same path and they did not want to end up another divorce statistic. The bottom line was Roger and Mary really didn't know where their money was going. They could not list with any certainty how much they spent on eating out, groceries, gasoline, or even Starbucks. During one of our visits we agreed that you couldn't get to where you want to go financially if you didn't know where you were. I asked Roger and Mary if they would both be willing to carry a 25-cent notebook in their pocket and write down every cash purchase they made for the next 30 days. They didn't like that idea at all. They were too busy; it just would not happen consistently. So I asked them if they could say, "May I have a receipt please?" They agreed that they could and every time they went to the store, coffee shop, or drive-thru they stuffed the receipt into a Starbucks cup in the center counsel of each car.

This chapter's activity: Save all of your receipts for 30 days and have a receipt totaling party at the end of the month. Use the form in this chapter to assist you.

You can also download this form at: www.budgetsthatwork.com/forms.

At the end of the 30 days Roger and Mary put the kids to bed, turned off the TV, made smoothies, and had a receipt totaling party. They dumped out the receipts on the living room rug and sorted them into piles. A gasoline pile here, a convenient store pile there, and so on. They were amazed at the dollars they spent especially when they totaled up the highest pile—Starbucks. Roger, the biggest offender, said, "How could we be spending $90 a month at Starbucks? That's over $1,000 a year. Something has to change." Mary was holding back from saying, "Let's total my Chai Tea Latte receipts and your Pike

Place and see who spends more." As a result they both decided to make premium coffee at home during the week to take with them in the morning. They also found they got to work on time more often. This was a painful sacrifice to them and they limited themselves to just going to Starbucks on Sundays, which was a ritual for them. After adding in the mid-week trips to the convenient stores, their spending on groceries was much higher than Mary originally thought. The food total really hurt when she added in the fast food receipts. "Perhaps I could do a better job of planning meals," Mary said.

Once you have your sorting party, you can insert your spending into the form titled "Monthly Income & Expenses by Category." This form is at the end of Chapter 6.

If you feel you may have missed collecting too many receipts, just try again for another 30 days. Don't worry about the other blanks on the form; we'll get to them later.

May I have a receipt please?
CASH SPENDING TRACKING FORM
Yes it is time to add up all those receipts you have been collecting for thirty days. Sort them into ten piles, one for each category below and add them up.

Category	Total for 30 days.
Housing	$
Auto	$
Entertainment	$
Clothing	$
Medical	$
Grocery Store	$
Take Out Food	$
Coffee Shop	$
Restaurants eat in	$
Miscellaneous	$
TOTAL	$

Where can you cut back? It is only temporary.

Print this form at www.budgetsthatwork.com/forms
From the book "The Unemployment Budget" Your financial survival plan by Patrick Mellody

CHAPTER 5
AM I WORTH MORE DEAD THAN ALIVE?

Frank and Jean are an interesting professional couple. They are true DINKS: Dual Income No Kids. They lived in an exclusive neighborhood on the island and drove a leased Mercedes. They vacationed several times per year with friends. How could they say no when everyone else was going?

Jean joked, "You know, Pat, Frank is worth more to me dead than alive". I was going to tell them that marriage counseling was not my thing when she explained that Franks' father died at a young age and left the family penniless. He had a very hard life growing up. Frank wanted to be sure his family never experienced this, so he had a $2,000,000 life insurance policy. Truly he was worth more dead than alive because in real life they made $350,000 per year and spent $407,500 per year, a problem many people would love to have. They had been so entrenched in a certain lifestyle; trying to keep up with friends who made more than they did, that it just happened. Frank was deep in debt and in denial. He needed to see it on paper before he could admit he had a problem.

This chapter's activity: Make a list of your debts and assets. Total them and see which is highest. Use the quick form in this chapter.

You can also download this form at: www.budgetsthatwork.com/forms.

Take a look at your assets. Is there anything you can sell that would help your situation? A toy or piece of property? You can always replace them later.

List Of Debts

Creditors Name	Phone Number	Pay off amount	# of payments left	Monthly Payment	Due Date	% of interest
	Total Debts					Total Payments

List of Assets	Current Value
Home	
Auto 1	
Auto 2	
RV	
Boat	
Motorcycle	
401K	
Stocks	
Bonds	
Savings	
Jewelry	
Land	
Other	
Home 2	
TOTAL	
Total Assets	
Total Debts	
Your Net Worth		Plus or Minus

Print this form at www.budgetsthatwork.com/forms

From the book "The Unemployment Budget" Your financial survival plan by Patrick Mellody

CHAPTER 6
WHERE AM I?

Tom was single and made a good living working for the Post Office. He worked a great deal of overtime. In fact, he made an extra $20,000 as a result. But all good things come to an end; even the Post Office is cutting back. The problem was Tom liked to travel during his several weeks of paid vacation. He liked it so much that he was over $60,000 in debt just in credit cards. He was always able to work some overtime and get caught up, but not anymore. Tom was a very visual person. He needed to see his monthly spending on a single page so it would sink in. Just being short $1,667 a month in overtime pay was a wake-up call. Tom was surprised when he totaled the bottom of the form and saw how much he was overspending every month.

This chapter's activity: Make a list of your monthly expenses and total them. Use the "Monthly Income & Expense by Category" form in this chapter. You might have already put some information in this form after you read Chapter 4. You can print this form at www.budgetsthatwork.com/forms.

Monthly Income & Expenses by Category

Current Net	
Take home Income	

Housing	Total	
Mortgage or	_____
Rent	_____
Insurance	_____
Taxes	
Electric	_____
Gas	_____
Water	_____
Garbage	_____
All Phones	
Internet	_____
TV Plan	_____
other	_____

Auto	Total	
Payments	_____
Gas & Oil	_____
Insurance	_____
License	_____
Register	_____
Repair	_____
Other	_____

Insurance	Total	
Life	_____
Medical	_____
Other	_____

Debts	Total	
Cards	_____
Loans	_____
Notes	_____
Personal	_____
Other	_____

Entertainment Total	
Eating out	_____
Baby Sitters	_____
Trips/Activities	_____
Vacation	_____
Other	_____
Other	_____

Clothing	Total	
Back to School	_____
Foot ware	_____
All Other	_____

Savings   Total

Medical Expenses	Total	
Doctor	
Dentist	_____
Prescriptions	_____
Vet	_____
Other	_____

Miscellaneous	Total	
Alcohol	
Tobacco	_____
Day Care	_____
Toiletry/cosmetics	_____
Beauty/Barber	_____
Laundry/Dry Cleaning	_____
Allowance/Lunches	_____
Subscriptions	_____
Gifts/Christmas	_____
Cash	_____
Dues/Organizations	_____
Other	_____

Food	Total	
Take out Drive Thru	_____
Groceries	_____

TOTAL EXPENSES

INCOME vs. EXPENSES

Net Take-home Income	
Less Total Expenses	
Surplus/Deficit	

Print this form at www.budgetsthatwork.com/forms
From the book "The Unemployment Budget" Your financial survival plan by Patrick Mellody

CHAPTER 7
IT'S LIKE FINDING NEW-FOUND MONEY!

I met with Tim and Mary twice. Tim lost his job after 16 years of dedicated service. Tim was making $65,000 per year and had been looking for a job for six months. They made significant progress filling out their forms. They had been tracking their spending and were surprised at some of their category spending totals. When they saw how much they were paying for services like cable, car insurance, cell phone/texting they knew they could do better. They were determined to live within their means or as financial guru Dave Ramsey says, they were willing to "act their wage." They made a plan of attack. They looked at every expense they had and went on a mission to see how they could reduce each and every one. Tim called three insurance companies for competing quotes on all their insurances. He found the best way to compare apples to apples was to take his current policies, white out the dollar amounts, and fax them over to the various companies. He asked them for pricing on the identical coverage. A little over a week went by and he plotted out the results on the kid's chalkboard. What a surprise, two of the companies were lower. One company was $356 per year lower. That's almost $30 per month! "I can pay my JC Penney bill with that," Mary said. Before they cancelled their current policy, they contacted their representative. They told their representative that they have enjoyed their business relationship and they would like to stay with them if they could match the competitors quote. The representative called them back the next day. Not only did he match the offer he suggested moving their deductible from $250 to $500 which made their total savings $480 per year. Encouraged by this new-found money, they followed the same process with cable, cell phone, and even daycare. They liked the children's daycare and really did not want to move them, but they were still able to negotiate a discount for pre-paying for the month and no late fees for picking up the kids late. Quite easily they found $149 per month of new-found money to put toward other bills.

This chapter's activity: Review your current bills, contact like providers, compare them and reduce your monthly expenses.

CHAPTER 8
WHAT IS A VARIABLE EXPENSE AND WHY SHOULD I CARE?

I worked on Ken and Nancy's budget for a long time. It wasn't coming together very well. It looked like they had plenty of money to make it through the month. Nancy filled in the blanks on the monthly expense form right out of her checkbook. We went over the form line by line and found some blanks. I asked her if she had any variable expenses and she said, "What is a variable expense and why should I care?" I explained that a variable expense was an expense that doesn't necessarily come due every month. Sometimes various insurance payments such as life, car, and home owners/renters come due two or four times per year. If your property and school taxes are not in escrow with your mortgage payment, you'll need to set this money aside every month so when the bills come in you have the funds to pay it promptly before any penalties. It's also a good idea to plan for "back to school" expenses. The kids go back to school every year and need hundreds of dollars worth of clothes and supplies, so why not prepare for that, also. Sure enough we found some variable expenses and divided them by 12 months and inserted the totals into the Monthly Expense form.

This chapter's activity is: Make a list of your expenses that do not come due every month, perhaps just quarterly. Use the easy quick form "Variable Expense Spending" found in this chapter. It can also be printed at www.budgetsthatwork.com/forms.

Variable Expenses Planning

Plan for those expenses that are not paid on a regular monthly basis by estimating the yearly cost and determining the average cost per month.			
	PER YEAR		Per Month
Doctor		DIVIDED	
Dentist		BY TWELVE	
Back to School		MONTHS EQUALS	
Auto Repair / Replace			
Insurance			
Life			
Auto			
Health			
Home or renters			
Clothing			
School Taxes not in escrow			
Home Taxes not in escrow			
Investments			
Other			
Other			
TOTAL	$		$

Print this form at www.budgetsthatwork.com/forms
From the book "The Unemployment Budget" Your financial survival plan by Patrick Mellody

16

CHAPTER 9
WHAT IS THE MAGIC FORMULA FOR SPENDING AND HOW DO I SIZE UP?

"No one ever told me how much I could afford to spend on cars, housing, or anything else, for that matter. Should I guess?" That was the question that Kate, a single mom, asked me. How right she was. I can't remember a single high school or college class that said, "As you get out there in the real world you should only spend 32% of your take-home income on housing, 14% on autos, and so on." Wouldn't that have been nice? Very few of us were ever taught how to handle money. Kate needed to find out where she was financially and try to fix it.

I have provided a spending guideline for every category in your Unemployment Budget. This guideline will allow you to compare your actual spending against the guide to see where any overspending issues are. The categories add up to 100% so please don't shoot the author if you aren't even close on some of the categories. I find that that the two most challenging categories are housing and auto. If these two categories are out of sync, some of the other categories must be lower than suggested. If this is not possible, you may have some hard decisions to make. I know it was not in your plans to be unemployed, but I hope you use this budget to make well-informed decisions. You worked hard for what you have and I know you want to keep everything, but we are talking survival here. If you exhaust every avenue and your house or autos are going to bankrupt you, remember, you had the income to purchase them once and you can do it again later.

This chapter's activity: Refer to the form in this chapter. Insert the requested information to realize what your "in a perfect world" spending should be. Remember, the percentages add up to 100% and that is all you have to spend. You can print this form at www.budgetsthatwork.com/forms.

How much should I be spending as a percentage of my take home income?

| | | | Enter Your Current Monthly Net Take-home Income | | |

MONTHLY PAYMENT CATEGORY	EXISTING MONTHLY SPENDING	IDEAL SPENDING PERCENTAGE OF YOUR TAKE-HOME INCOME	IDEAL SPENDING AMOUNT	DIFFERENCE PLUS OR MINUS	NEW MONTHLY TARGET BUDGET
**Example: Housing	$1,500	32%	$1,280	$220 over	$1,280
Housing		32%			
Auto		14%			
Insurance		5%			
Debts		5%			
Entertainment		5%			
Clothing		5%			
Savings		5%			
Medical		6%			
Miscellaneous		9%			
Food		14%			
TOTALS		100%			

** Example of Housing with a take-home income of $4000.00 per month. $4000.00 X 32% = $1,280.00 but this couple spends $1,500.00 , they are overspending by $220.00 per month. If you need to reduce spending see chapter 5.
Note: Fill in the dollar amounts you calculated from the "Monthly Income & Expense by Category" form.

From the book "The Unemployment Budget" Your financial survival plan by Patrick Mellody
Print this form at www.budgetsthatwork.com/forms

CHAPTER 10
YOU MEAN I DON'T GET TO SPEND IT ALL?

Over the course of a summer, I taught a very basic finance class to young adults in the inner city of Buffalo, NY. This group of high school kids was amazed that taxes and other deductions would be coming out of their paychecks as they found jobs. One boy was so upset that he said, very puzzled, "You mean I don't get to spend it all?" I also get a similar response from adults. Frank and Sandra said, "Together we make $100,000 per year. Why shouldn't we be able to afford what we want? We work hard; we deserve it." I kindly told them that in the ideal situation we should spend less than we make and save some money. If we have some savings for emergencies, we can stop the use of credit cards and we all know emergencies happen quite often.

I looked at Frank and Sandra's paychecks, did the math, and found that they really brought home a net spendable income of $75,500. Our spending on each category of life should be figured against this lower spendable amount since this is really what we have to spend. Unless your state is an exception, your unemployment check is taxable income. Please be sure to use this take-home number to work with.

Sandra said something I hear all too often. "Well, the bank told us we could afford 38% of our income for a house payment." I explained that the percentage should be closer to 32% of their take-home income plus that amount should include utilities, escrow, and maintenance. Frank could see that the rest of their budget plan would not work because they were overspending on their home. When you only have 100% to spend and you're not drastically under-spending in another category, you are headed somewhere you don't want to go.

This chapter's activity: Calculate your Take Home Spendable Income." Use the quick form in this chapter. You can print this form at www.budgetsthatwork.com/forms.

NOTE: If you already completed the "Crisis Budget" from Chapter 3, you already completed this chapter's activity.

Calculate your Take-Home Income

1) Calculate your monthly take-home income BEFORE the loss of any Job or Jobs.		2) Deduct the amount of take-home income lost.		3) Subtract Total #1 from Total #2 and see your monthly income before Unemployment and other assistance.	
Job 1	$	Job 1	$		
Job 2	$	Job 2	$		
Other income	$	Other income	$		
Other income	$	Other income	$		
Total #1	$	Total #2	$	$	Total #3

4) Enter your take-home income fro

Unemployment	$	
Severance	$	
Food Stamps	$	
Other Assistance	$	
Other new income	$	
Total	$	Total #4

** Your New Monthly Take-Home Income:	$	Total of #3 + #4

Print this form at www.budgetsthatwork.com/forms

From the book "The Unemployment Budget" Your financial survival plan by Patrick Mellody

CHAPTER 11
CLEAR OFF THE KITCHEN TABLE AND PUT IT ALL TOGETHER.

You have done a great job of getting this far. Now it's time to see if all of your information is complete. You should have six forms in front of you that make up the Unemployment Budget. If you're like most people I talk with, there are some things you haven't done yet. Usually they are a little harder or they require some research. Well, this is the point where you say to yourself, "Self, you've invested too much in this process to stop. You've stopped before, but not this time. I'm determined to survive this season of life. I must keep going." Continue on after you complete the blanks on the six forms, you are so close.

Congratulations! You have all the information you need from the previous chapters to easily analyze your situation and put together a survival plan. In the work you did in the previous chapters you should have entered some information into the "Monthly Income and Expense by Category" form found at the end of Chapter 6.

If you haven't already, enter in your cash spending totals from Chapter 4.

Enter in your debts from Chapter 5.

Enter in your new lower totals from your adjusted bills that you worked on in Chapter 7.

Enter in your variable spending from Chapter 8.

Enter in your take-home income from Chapter 10.

Add up the totals for Housing, Auto, Insurance, Debts, Entertainment, Clothing, Savings, Medical Expenses, Miscellaneous, and Food. Place that total in the "Total Expense" box at the bottom right of the form. Subtract your total expenses from your take home income to see your surplus or deficit.

If you are like most people on unemployment I speak with, you spend more than you make. Put a check mark next to every item on the "Monthly Income & Expense by Category" form that you researched and reduced your spending to the lowest possible amount. If you missed some, re-read Chapter 7 and lower your expenses. Once you have cut out the luxuries and reduced your expenses I hope you have a surplus, but chances are you don't. If that is the case, we have a little more work to do. Hang in there. On the form, circle your total spending for Housing, Auto and Food. Add them up and write it down on the side of the form. These categories are what you need to protect first. Think of it as financial triage. Subtract this total from your net take-home income. Whatever is left is what you can pay towards your other bills, but I encourage setting aside some savings for when the car breaks or the fridge quits. If you don't have savings, you'll have to use credit and you really don't want to do that right now.

If you have bills that will remain unpaid, I know a non-profit organization that can help you— CredAbility. I mentioned CredAbility in Chapter 3: The Crisis Budget. In case you jumped right to the "Unemployment Budget," I'll fill you in. CredAbility is a non-profit organization that has a relationship with all the major creditors and can, in most cases, reduce your interest rates and work with you to develop a DMP or Debt Management Plan. They don't have a magic wand to make your debts go away, but they can help. Their web site is www.credability.org click on "Our Services" and then "Debt Management Plan". Watch the short video explaining the service. If you decide to work with them the forms in this book will make the process go much faster. As I mentioned previously I have referred dozens of people to this organization and they helped them survive and then thrive. You can also call them at 1-800-251-2227. CredAbility also has services such as Foreclosure Prevention and if you are far short of even your basic needs they offer Bankruptcy Education. Please exhaust all the referral services at the end of this book before considering bankruptcy. It is the last resort and unlike they say on TV it will not make all your problems go away, it will just start new ones. CredAbility is a non-profit agency but they do have an average charge of $35 to set up your account and a maximum charge of $50 if you have a lot going on that takes extra administrative time. It's the best money you'll ever spend and you'll save it back right away with the services they provide. CredAbility does stress that they are not a debt settlement company. They suggest that you contact your creditors directly if you have cash funds available to settle your debt for a reduced amount and close the account. They do not suggest paying some other TV advertised company to do what you can do yourself.

Let's look back at my promises from the beginning of the book. I stated that:

• You'll have a complete understanding of where your money is going on a monthly basis.

• You'll know exactly how much you are over/under spending in every category of life. Housing, food, auto and so on. You'll also know how much you are over/under spending totally per month and what to do about it.

• You'll have found "New Money" saved from adjusting your spending habits.

• You'll be provided a web site where you can download all the forms in this book for no charge.

• If you just have too many bills that you cannot pay, I will provide solid contact information to a non-profit organization I have recommended dozens of times that will help you work out a Debt Management Plan to relieve your financial stress.

• You'll discover how to survive this temporary season of life.

So there you are. You are to be congratulated for taking a big step forward. We all eventually have to pay back what we borrow but I hope you'll find that the information in this book will keep you going until you secure your next job.

In conclusion, I want to share some personal thoughts with you. I've been unemployed several times in my life. I was only financially prepared for unemployment once and that was when I was laid off in 2009. I must tell you that the time before that, in 2002, was extremely rough. I worked for a great company with people I really enjoyed for 16 years. I had 8 months notice that my job was going away and that was still not enough to find something even close. Even though this company was extremely helpful and I still keep in touch with my friends there to this day, I was not prepared financially or mentally for unemployment. When you love what you do, you take pride in your work. You also take pride in providing for your family. When that is taken from you it can affect you. I know what it is like to be stressed out and become depressed. If it wasn't for my wife and a reminder of my faith, I don't know if I would have pulled out of it. If you are at that low point in life I want to tell you that you are special, you are unique. You are here on this earth for a special purpose. I want you to be especially hopeful because if I can go from being a guy that didn't even balance his checkbook to being a guy that currently has no debt, you can too. It was not easy to get out of debt and pay off all my bills, and any slick TV ads that tell you it is are lying. I followed the same information that you have in this book. It works and you'll succeed.

My goal in writing this book was to help you as I was helped. I made this book available for the same price as a couple of cups of Starbucks coffee so anyone could purchase it. As you work through this season of your life I want to hear your success story. I hope you email me. Hearing your story would be a great encouragement to me. (patrick@budgetsthatwork.com) I have provided some referral services to assist through this unemployment season. They are separated by faith-based and non-faith based—you choose what is right for you.

A Special Word to Returning and Retired Military Men and Women

If you are a returning military person that is looking for work I wish I had a business where I could hire all of you. My family and I are forever in your debt for serving our country and allowing me the time and freedom to write this book. I do not pretend to understand the unique financial circumstances you are facing and I would appreciate hearing from you so I can gather some information for my next project. I will be tailoring a budget book for returning and unemployed military families. I will make the new book available along with any helpful links you can pass on to me for free as a small appreciation of my gratitude. Please e-mail me at the link provided on my website. We'll write this new book together and with your permission I'll add your name, rank, and unit as a contributor to the book.

It's time to get to work. You are another day closer to your next job!

Referral Services

www.credability.org 1-800-251-2227 CredAbility is non-profit agency founded in 1964. They will help you lower your interest rates and create a Debt Management Plan. CredAbility also offers counseling on Foreclosure Prevention, Bankruptcy Education and Reverse Mortgages. They also offer budget and credit counseling. Check out the education section for videos on dozens of topics. This site receives the author's 5 Star Rating.

www.995hope.org 1-888-995-HOPE (4673) 24hr. hotline. Homeowners Hope Hotline is a non-profit agency that offers advice and support on foreclosure prevention. They are a HUD certified organization.

www.annualcreditreport.com Be sure to type in this full address to get to the proper site. 1-877-322-8228 This site allows you to request a free credit file disclosure, commonly called a credit report, once every 12 months from each of the nationwide consumer credit reporting companies: Equifax, Experian and TransUnion.

www.bankrate.com Bank Rate compares rates on mortgages, credit cards, CDs, money markets, and various loan products.

www.irs.gov/advocate Helps the taxpayer resolve problems with the IRS.

National Suicide Prevention Hotline: 1-800- 273-TALK (8255) 24-hour confidential hotline. No matter how bad your financial situation is, take the time to talk it out with a caring person from this great service. You'll be glad you did.

CareerNavigatorProgram.com: A Program for Job Search Survival & Success. A 5-day interactive, strategic approach to proactively managing a career now and in the future. danhoward3@gmail.com

FAITH-BASED REFERRAL SERVICES

www.newhopenow.org New Hope Telephone Counseling Center: 24-hour counseling services

1-714-NEW-HOPE (639-4673) Suicide Prevention Hotline. Caring people are waiting to talk to you.

www.intouch.org/resources/all-things-are-new Dr. Charles Stanley of In Touch Ministries posts 24 faith-based encouraging videos plus a free download titled "Overcoming Discouragement".

www.crossroadscareer.org Crossroads Career Network helps people find jobs, careers and callings, with online resources and career groups. For a limited time download a free copy of their 80-page workbook, which includes over 200 career resources. This site receives the author's 5 Star Rating.

www.crown.org Crown Financial Ministries 1-800-722-1976. For 35 years this non-profit ministry has assisted thousands, including the author, with in-person or online financial coaching. They offer more free online resources than I can mention here. Be sure to see the Crown Money Map.

www.careerdirectonline.org The Career Direct® Complete Guidance System is an individual, personal growth resource designed to help you maximize your God-given talents and abilities. More than a simple career test, it analyzes four critical areas: personality, interests, skills, and values. Most other career assessments only analyze one or two.

www.medi-share.org Medi-Share, Christian Family Healthcare 1-800-772-5623

www.family.org Focus on the Family - your one-stop resource for anything to do with the family—life changes, parenting, and marriage information.

www.ingramcontent.com/pod-product-compliance
Lightning Source LLC
Chambersburg PA
CBHW051430200326
41520CB00023B/7423